Poodle, Poodle Training
But Don't Eat Your P...
Training | Here's EXACTLY How to Train Your Poodle

By Paul Allen Pearce

Copyright © 2014 Paul Allen Pearce

The Poodle

The Poodle is a very old dog breed that was developed in Germany for hunting waterfowl and later the French developed it into the distinct breed we call the Poodle. In fact, the actual pilgrimage to Germany is a little hazy, but Poodles have a long history and varied crossbred heritage, one, being the North African Barbet that ended up in Gaul where it was primarily used for its hunting abilities. Whichever the exact route the poodle took is not crystal clear. Poodle type dogs are represented in Egyptian and Roman art verifying some of their ancient historical voyage.

Poodles come in three sizes, standard, miniature, and toy. It is known that sometime in the 1400's Parisians began to make smaller versions to delight the Parisian bourgeoisie. The miniature was followed by the toy and this was done by breeding Poodles to each other not by crossbreeding. The Standard Poodle was used for duck hunting, the Miniature for sniffing out yummy truffles in the woodlands, and the Toy was strictly for companionship within the upper classes of France. The name 'sleeve dog' when referring to Toy Poodles stems from wealthy Renaissance owners carrying them around inside their large shirtsleeves. I am sure it was all the rage.

Traveling performers and Gypsies took note of the intelligent and capable Poodle and put it to use performing tricks, also at times costumed for the crowds delight. Happy, friendly, intelligent, funny, and silly dogs, Poodles are great for families, as companions, and for therapy dogs. They love being in the spotlight and will be happy to perform and clown, and solve difficult calculus problems.

Well, maybe not calculus, but they are cunning. Other activities they enjoy and excel are agility, obedience, tracking, and herding. They have a long history of receiving top honors in shows and competitions.

Did I mention that they do well with children? They do well with children but remember the Toy Poodle is very small and can easily be injured by rough child play, please always keep an eye on your children no matter which breed or size they are playing.

The Poodles appearance by hair cut can be very entertaining. Poodle owners like to style their dog's coats into all sorts of craziness and elegance. The unique texture of their hair can be manipulated, and groomed into a myriad of stylish fashion, as well as some head scratchers. If you look, you will find a Poodle with an amusing haircut. Poodles have a single instead of double coat, comprised of dense, curly fur that sheds minimally. Their coats are moisture resistant and come in many colors, including black, white, blue, grey, silver, brown, café-au-lait, cream, and apricot.

Poodles are not heavy shedders and the hair that sheds gets caught up in the rooted hair. This keeps dog hair from getting on and around your house, but makes grooming a bit tiresome. Without proper grooming your Poodles hair will become matted and unruly. Exotic show clips take up as much as ten hours of grooming per week, then usually sheared off at the end of competition. A regular pet clip will be much more manageable and less time consuming.

On average, a Poodle should be groomed every six to eight weeks and this can be done at home.

Poodles have a few health concerns to which they are prone. Addison's disease, gastric dilatation volvulus (bloat/torsion), thyroid issues, tracheal collapse, epilepsy, sebaceous adadenitis, juvenile renal disease, hip dysplasia, and cancer. Keep a close watch in their ears and eyes.

Standard Poodles need their daily walks, but do not need strenuous exercise in abundance; however, they require more exercise than the two smaller breeds. The Standards are athletic, showing great stamina. They love the water so do not be surprised if you are out and they dive into a pond, pool, or ocean. The Standard will appreciate an open area run and stay in better health if given the opportunity to run and play. Miniature Poodles also require daily walks to keep them in optimal health, also appreciating further exercise in play and running. The Toy Poodle needs and appreciates the same as both its big brothers and sisters, but in smaller doses. That said; do not be surprised at the little Toy Poodles energy.

Training your Poodle will probably be an easy task as long as you establish your alpha position early displaying that you are in charge and humans are the top of the food chain. Poodles need to keep their brains working; this keeps them from destructive behaviors. Obedience training is perfect for this and an absolute necessity to keep your Poodles highly intelligent mind active and engaged. Their playful nature and fun loving ways need to be directed in positive ways. If you keep your Poodle occupied with training, games or sport, and exercise, the rest is a breeze. Try a game of chess occasionally, and see how you fair. *~Enjoy your Poodle dog!*

Introduction

Who is "man's best friend?" My wife says it's the couch, a pizza and ESPN, but that's because she grew up with four brothers. However, we all know man's best friend is his dog. I love my dog. I love dogs. They provide comfort, support, undying love, and someone to bounce all those brilliant ideas off that are going to make you a millionaire someday. I cannot imagine life without my dog.

When I picked Axel up and brought him home, he was a puppy. I was advised to train him well and not to make him a guard or an attack dog. Actually, training your dog makes him happier, healthier, and much more stable. Who knew?

With that in mind, I embarked on the journey of training this little puppy. Diving in head first, I bought books, acquired videos, and even talked with professional trainers about the matter. Over time, I gleaned a lot of helpful information. I learned about commonly encountered behavioral problems, and some not so common as well. I absorbed facts about proper diet, exercise, and training techniques. Because of my interest and commitment to his best interest, my dog is well behaved, happy, social, and understands a point spread better than any other dog traveling in the car pool lane.

While I was going through the process of learning how to train my puppy, I noticed one thing; trainers are really, really, serious about their craft, but will my lack of seriousness result in a poorly trained dog? The informality of my approach has resulted in a fabulous companion that clumsily bumps around the house, and chews on this and that in pure puppy form. Whether he's curled up snoozing or striking an adorable pose, the real joy comes simply from his mere presence, and of these joys, the laughter that he incites is at the very top of the list.

Keeping laughter and light heartedness in mind as a dog owner in training, is of the utmost importance because sometimes training can be very difficult on you and your pal. Sometimes your dog will push your patience to the limits. Remember to try and never let your dog know that you are at your limits. You are given the awesome responsibility at the time of acquisition, to be the pack leader and ultimately your dog's sensei.

I kept that in mind when I sat down to put this rewards based training book together. What I hope you will find inside here is a complete, concise training guide, the information of which is culled from trainers, training manuals and years of experience with a wonderful dog. Though this guide approaches training as a serious endeavor, your dog will teach you that it will not always be serious, and nor should you. I have attempted to infuse his playful spirit throughout this instructional. I hope that those light moments within this reading will help you get through the tougher times, like the chewing of your cell phone, the pooping on your socks and those mysterious expenses charged to your credit card. "Could be that only Axel is able to run a credit card via telephone."

A dog can be a loyal and longtime friend, worthy of your commitment and care. Your dog can give your life so much richness, and in return, asks very little. If you train him well, he or she will be happier, and as science has proven, so will you. If you keep a sense of humor alive during training, the outcomes will be the best for both of you. I hope you find this guide informative, easy to follow and fun. Enjoy.

Table of Contents

Getting Social with Your Poodle ___ 8

Rewards, Not Punishment ___ 13

Training, Here Are Some Things That Work ___ 15

Clicker Training Your Poodle is Key ___ 19

Let's Talk Treats ___ 21

PART II: Let's Go To School ___ 23

"Come", this command is important too ___ 25

"Drop it" – A must for all dog owners ___ 28

"Leave it", as opposed to "Drop it" ___ 31

Let's Sit ___ 33

Handle Me Gently ___ 34

    Handling Different Areas of the Dog's Body ___ 35

Going Out On a 'Leash' Here ___ 39

Supine Time (Lie Down) ___ 44

"Stay" (Just a Little Bit Longer) ___ 45

Go West Young Dog, or, Wherever Else I Point You ___ 47

Nipping, Yep, the Ole Nipperdoggie ___ 49

Jumping Jeepers ___ 51

House Training ___ 55

Care and Goals, Being a Good Human to Your Dog ___ 58

Barking Madness	63
Body Language and Vocals	69
Dog Treating	75
Dog Nutrition	79
Raw Food Stuff	80
Human Foods for Dogs	83
That's All Folks	91
About the Author	96
Poodle Facts	99
Other Books	104

Getting Social with Your Poodle

Socializing, especially before the age of six months, is a very important step in preventing behavior problems. Socializing can and should continue through the life of your dog. Socializing, gently, and kindly, prevents aggressive, fearful, and sometimes litigious behavior. A lack of socializing may lead to aggressive behavior, barking, shyness, hyperactivity, (and possibly wearing Goth make up.) The earlier you start socializing the better. However, all Poodles' can gradually be brought into new and initially fearful situations, eventually learning to enjoy them.

Socializing your dog is a lifelong endeavor. If your Poodle does not see other dogs for months or years at a time, you would expect his behavior to be different when he encounters them again. I mean, how would you feel if your sixth grade math teacher, who you haven't seen in 22 years, just walked up to you and sniffed you?

Here are some ways to expose your Poodle to something new or something he was distrustful with

- You must remain calm, upbeat and keep his leash loose if he has one on.

- Expose him gradually; never force him to face what he is wary. Let him retreat if he needs to. If it gets very serious and his forehead begins to sweat, let him phone a friend.

- Reward him using treats for being calm and exploring new situations, a good scratch, or a long run.

Try to expose your dog to the things you would like him to be able to cope with on a regular basis. This will allow him to deal with such situations calmly in the future. Be careful of exposing him to the same things over again, becoming routine, the same old, same old. Maybe I don't want to go to the same place every single year for vacation. This exposure may seem tedious but it will pay off with a well-behaved dog.

Here are some examples of situations but the list goes on

- Meeting new people of all kinds, including but not limited to, children, crowds, people wearing hats, disabled, and people in local services such as post, fire/police officers, and so forth.

- *Meeting new dogs* (Especially new puppies). Be careful here, because of disease, wait 4 months before you bring your puppy to areas with many dogs). Exposure to other pets; such as cats, horses, birds, llamas, pigs and so forth.

- Teach him to enjoy his crate. We will be going over instructions in a later chapter.

- *Riding in the car* –Again please get in this habit early on. Be sure you restrain him properly with a secure crate strapped in with a seatbelt, or use a specific dog seatbelt or similar.

- Being touched, held, and petted all over, in different ways. Being bathed and groomed, *as well as being admired from afar.*

- Visiting the vet's office, groomer, day care, and boarding kennel.

- Expose him to loud noises and strange objects.

- Expose him to traffic while leash training e.g. motorcycles, bicycles, skateboards, joggers etc.

- Get him used to being alone for a few hours at a time. Maybe leave the radio or TV on to keep him company. Always have a couple of his or her favorite chew toys handy to work out that separation aggression.

Well That's Not Good Behavior

How to deal with problem behavior before it becomes a habit

Everyone likes their own space to feel comfy, familiar, and safe. Your dog is no different. A proper living space is a key factor to avoiding all kinds of problems. Think of all the things your Poodle will encounter in his life with humans; baths, walks, radio, T.V., neighbors, visitors, the vacuum, and so forth and that these *things* are not common and frightening. Use treats, toys, and praise to assist you in training and socializing.

Communicate with your dog. Communication is always the key. If he sees his good, calm behavior is frequently rewarded and that you have control of his favorite things (toys/treats) this is a gateway to solving problems that may arise down the road.

Keep your dog's world happy. Make sure he is getting a proper amount of exercise and be sure that he is being challenged mentally. Make sure he is getting enough time in the company of other dogs and other people. Keep a close eye on his diet, good, healthy foods. Treat now and then, but go easy, and keep them tiny.

It is important that you be a strong leader, your dog needs to know that you are the boss. Do not let 'situations' fall into that questionable who's the boss scenario. Your puppy will feel confident and strong if he works for his rewards. Let him show you good behavior before you pile on the goodies, a bonus round of treats, his dinner, or a new roof on his doghouse. He will appreciate it more.

Getting by the challenges

Your dog's first step in overcoming the challenges of life, is understanding his own behavior and what motivates it. Some behaviors your dog will engage in, is instinctual. Barking, chewing, jumping, digging, and leash pulling, are things that all dogs do because it is in their genetic make-up. These natural behaviors differ from the ones we have inadvertently trained into our dogs. Behaviors such as barking for attention or nudging our hands asking to be petted are accidently trained by us.

What motivates your dog to do what he does or does not do? Why, you may wonder, does he not come when you call him when he is playing with other dogs? This may be because coming to you is far less exciting than scrapping with other dogs. Change this by offering a highly coveted treat or letting him continue to play for a while. Start slow and in short distances [Key].

Here are some helpful tips to use when trying to help your Poodle through challenging behavior.

- Think about his diet and health. Is your dog getting enough play time, mental exercise and sleep? Is this a medical problem? *Could he be right*? Do not ignore the possibilities.

- Are you accidentally rewarding bad behavior? Remember that your dog may see ANY response as a reward. You can ignore the misbehavior if you are patient enough, or you can give your Poodle the equivalent of a "time out" for a few minutes. Make sure the time out is in a calm, quiet and safe but very dull place, much like my grandmothers condo in Florida.

- Practice replacement behavior. For example, if your dog jumps up to get love, teach him to sit instead. Reward him with something that is much more appealing than misbehaving. It is important what you ask your dog for, and *reward, his good behavior* before he misbehaves.

- While practicing the replacement behavior, be sure you reward the right response and ignore the mistakes. Any response to the mistake could be mistaken as a reward by your dog. Start slowly and easily, beginning with the stuff that your dog can succeed with; sitting, staying, coming when you call, then progress onto things that are more difficult.

- Your dog's bad behavior may be caused by something that he finds scary. If this is the case, try to change his mind. Pair the scary thing with something he loves. Say your dog has a problem with the Mail carrier. Pair the Mail Carrier's visit with a super treat and lots of attention. He will soon look forward to the post person's visits. He may even ask neighborhood kids to dress up like the mail carrier; in this case, you may have done the replacement behavior too well.

- Always, be patient with your dog and do not force changes. Work gradually and slowly. Forcing behavioral changes on your dog may lead to worse behavior.

~ Paws On – Paws Off ~

Rewards, Not Punishment

It is always better to reward your dog rather than punishing him. Here are a few reasons why.

- If you punish your Poodle, it can make him distrust, fear, and avoid you. If you rub your dog's nose in it, he may avoid going to the bathroom in front of you. This is going to make his life difficult in public.

- Electric fences will make him avoid the yard and choke collars can cause injuries to his throat as well as cause back and neck misalignment.

- Physical punishment has the tendency to escalate. If you get your dog's attention by a light tap on the nose, he will soon get used to that and ignore it. Soon the contact will become more and more violent. As we know, violence is NOT the answer.

- Punishing your dog may have some bad side effects. For example if you are using a pinch collar, it may tighten when he encounters other dogs. Now, we know your dog is smart, but he isn't always logical. The pinching of the collar when your dog encounters another dog may lead him to think the other dog is the reason for the pinch. Pinch collars have been known to cause aggression toward other dogs.

- You may inadvertently develop and adversarial relationship with your dog if you punish him instead of working through rewards. If you only look for the mistakes in your dog, this is all you will see. In your mind, you will see a problem dog. In your puppy's mind, he will see anger and distrust.

- You ultimately want to change your dog's bad behavior into good behavior. By punishing your dog, he will learn only to *avoid* punishment. He is not learning to change or to be good, he is learning to be sneaky or to do the very minimum simply to avoid being punished.

- If you punish rather than reward neither you nor your dog will be having a very good time. It will be a constant, sometimes painful struggle. If you have children, they will not be able to participate in a punishment based training process because it is too difficult.

- Simply put, if you train your dog using rewards, you and your dog will have a much better time. Rely on rewards to change his behavior by using treats, toys, playing, petting, affection, or anything else you know your dog likes. If your dog is doing something you do not like, replace the habit with another by teaching him to do something different and then reward him and enjoy.

~ Paws On – Paws Off ~

Training, Here Are Some Things That Work

Knowing what you want to train your dog to do is as important as training your dog. You can begin training almost immediately, around six weeks of age. A puppy is a blank slate and does not know any rules, therefore it is a wise idea to make a list and have an understanding of what you would like your puppy to do. As he grows, the same principle applies and you may adjust training from the basics to further topics such as making your dog a good travel, hiking, agility, hunting, or simply a companion dog. Know what conditions and circumstances you plan to expose your dog or puppy outside of the household and strategize to be prepared for those encounters by slowly socializing him to those situations.

Establish yourself as the pack leader from the time you first bring your new dog or puppy home. Being the 'alpha' assists in training and your relationship you, your dog, and family will have. Life is easier for your dog if you are in charge. Leading as the alpha assists in working together with your dog towards the goal of understanding the rules of conduct and obedience. Your dog will be at ease when the rules are understood. Training should be an enjoyable bonding time between you and your dog. Remember that there is no set time limit to when your dog should learn and understand commands then obey. Use short training sessions and be aware that if either of you are tired, to quit and try it again later or a different day. If something, does not seem quite right with your dog learning or behaving, have him checked out by a veterinarian.

Timing is crucial – Rewards or corrections need to be made immediately after the action. ***Patience and Consistency*** – are your allies in the training game. Remember to give your dogs or puppies their daily exercise to keep them fit, healthy, and behavioral problems at bay. Provide consistent structure, firm authority, rule enforcement, love and affection, and you will have one heck of a companion and friend. Reward good behaviors, but do not reward for being cute, sweet, loveable, and huggable. If you wish to reward your dog, always reward after you issue and your dog obeys a command such as "Sit". Keep your training sessions short, mix it up, and add a variety of treats and rewards. Relax, have fun, and enjoy the process of bonding and training your dog or puppy.

- TREATS, We all love them, so does your Poodle. Giving your dog a treat is the best way to reinforce good behavior, help change his behavior or just make him do that insanely funny dance like thing he does. Make the treats small, enough for him to get a taste, not a meal. You do not want him filling up on treats it might spoil his dinner.

- Keep a container of treats handy all the time, you don't want to miss a chance to reward good behavior or reinforce a changed behavior. Always carry treats on a walk. Remember the treats your dog likes most and save those for super special times. In addition, what you consider a treat and what your dog considers a treat are two vastly different worlds. Single malt scotch or chicken wings … Not a good treat for your puppy.

- Ask for something before you give the treat. Tell your dog to sit, stay, and lie down, print two copies of your resume, anything, before you reward him with snacks, petting, or play. By asking for good behavior, before you give him a reward you demonstrate you are in charge in an easy, fun manner. There is a common misconception that dogs are selfless, should behave only to please and out of respect and not for treats. This is horsepucky. This line of thinking is very wrong. You have to make sure your dog knows exactly WHY he should listen to you ... Because you are the keeper of the treats, the provider of the scratching and the purveyor of toys.

- Be positive. Think about what you want your dog to 'Do' instead of what you 'Don't' want him to do. Ignore the bad behavior so you do not send mixed messages and reward him when he does what you want him to DO. Teach your dog some simple words to communicate what you want, "drop it", or "Leave it". Simple things he can learn with ease.

- Keep the training sessions short, 15 minutes maximum per session. You will always be training your dog but use the formal training sessions to focus on one thing. Anything longer than 15 minutes it will be hard for him to focus.

- Your dog will be much happier if you run him every day. Run your dog till his tongue is hanging out. If he is still antsy or hyperactive, run him again.

- Kids are great, aren't they? However, the notion that kids and dogs are as natural a pairing as chocolate and peanut butter is just not true. Kids are often bitten by dogs because they accidently do things that frighten dogs or even make themselves seem like prey. Never leave a dog and a child unsupervised, even if the dog is 'good' with children. Teach children not to approach a dog that is unfamiliar to them. The way a child behaves with the familiar, family dog, may not fly with another dog they meet for the first time.

- It is very important that you make sure your dog is comfortable in all sorts of situations. All dogs, even your sweet tempered dog, have the potential to bite. Making sure, he is comfortable in various situations and teaching him to be gentle with his mouth will reduce the risk of unwanted bites.

~ Paws On – Paws Off ~

Clicker Training Your Poodle is Key

What the heck is that clicking noise? Well, It's, it's a clicker, thus the name. If you are a product of a Catholic school, you might be very familiar with this device. You probably have nightmares of large, penguin like women clicking their way through your young life. Yes, it was annoying and at times, terrifying. However, when it comes to training your Poodle, it will be helpful and fun.

The clicker is used to inform your dog he did the right thing AND that a treat is coming. When your dog does the right thing, like drop your Chanel purse dangling from his mouth, you click and reward him with a nice treat. Using the clicker system allows you to set your dog up to succeed while you ignore or prevent bad behavior. It is a very positive system and punishment is not part of the process.

Here are some questions often asked about the clicker training.

- Why wouldn't you give a verbal reward instead of clicking? You can certainly say; good, yes, well done, how delightful, who's a smarty-pants or any other positive verbal reward, but the clicker is generally much faster.

- Do I need to have the clicker on me at all times? No. The clicker is a learning tool. Once your dog understands what you want him to do, you can then use a verbal or hand reward marker. See above for verbal rewards.

- With all these treats, isn't he going to get fat? No. If you figure treats into your dog's daily intake, not as something extra, he should be fine. The treats should be small, just a taste. Use food from his meal when you are training indoors, but when outdoors, use fresh treats like meat and cheese. There are many distractions outside and a tasty fresh treat will help keep your Poodle's attention.

- Can rewards be other things besides treats? Sure. Actually, you should mix it up. Use the clicker and a treat when you first start teaching. When your dog has learned the behavior you want, and then switch to other rewards, petting, play, lottery tickets ... *Remember* to always ask for a behavior such as 'sit', 'stay', or 'come' before you reward your dog.

- What do I do if my dog disobeys a command? If your dog disobeys you it is because he has not been properly trained. Sorry, but you have to take the responsibility for that. He, after all, is just a dog. You, on the other hand, have a driver's license. If he is disobeying, he has not been taught well enough or the treat is not good enough. Make the task simpler and clearer, and make the reward equal to, or better than what he is being distracted.

HELPFUL HINT

- *Be sure NOT* to show your dog the treat before you click. If you do this, he will be responding to the treat and not the click and this will *undermine* training.

~ Paws On – Paws Off ~

Let's Talk Treats

So, you're training your Poodle and he is doing well, of course, because he is the best dog in the world, yes he is yes he is ... But you want to make sure you're giving him the right kind of treats. Treats are easy. As long as you stay away from the things that aren't good for dogs; Avocado, onions and garlic, in any form, coffee, tea or caffeine, grapes, raisins, macadamia nuts, peaches, plums, pits, persimmons or chocolate, whiskey soda, Guinness Stout ... to name a few.

You can make a treat from many foods. Treats should be small, corn nut sized, and easy to grab from a pocket or container. When you are outdoors and there are many distractions, treats should be better quality, cubes of cheese, dried meat, and such. Make sure you *mix them up*, Nothing is worse for treat training than your dog turning his nose up at a treat because he has had it too often.

Here are some treat ideas:

- Cubed meats

- Shredded cheese... Dogs love cheese and ...well, you know the rest

- Cream cheese, peanut butter, or easy cheese. Give your dog a lick for every proper behavior.

- Cereal, Cheerios is good, no milk, no bowl, and no spoon, just the goods

- Kibble (dry foods). Put some in a paper bag and smell it up with some bacon or other meat.

- Beef Jerky

- Carrot or apple pieces

- Meat baby food, you know those little suspect sausage things. You would cry too c'mon now.

- Commercial dog treats. Careful here, there are tons of them on the market. Look for those that do not have preservatives, by products, or artificial colors.

- Ice cube. Not the rapper, the frozen water treats. Yup, your dog will love crunching these up.

Avoid feeding your hairy friend from the table; you do not want to teach him to beg when people are sitting down at the table. Make sure treats are given far from the dinner table, not wherever people are gathering to eat.

~ *Paws On – Paws Off* ~

PART II: Let's Go To School

Now we are going to teach your dog some specific things. Let us start with a base exercise, getting your dog to respond to his *name*. I assume you have named your puppy and now you want him to learn his name. This can be easy and fun.

- Get a nice variety of treats and put them in your pockets, treat pouch or on a tabletop. When your puppy looks at you, say his name…Give him a treat. When he is more advanced, you could also use quarters and let your puppy get his own treats from a vending machine.

- Seriously, this is the most important behavior and it is going to form the base of all the other things you will be teaching him later on. Therefore, you will want to spend the time and give this a considerable amount of attention. Repeat the exercise all over the house while he is on the leash, outside in the yard, in the park. Make sure you practice this while there are distractions such as guests in the house, his favorite toys visible, food around, and other dogs.

-Call your puppy's name, get eye contact, and give him a treat. This is going to avoid trouble later on down the line. If your puppy gets into something he should not; a scrap with another puppy, chasing a cat or squirrel, a time-share pyramid scheme, you call his name and he will come for the treat, and later he will come only because you command it.

- It may sound odd, but also try to doing this when you are in different positions such as sitting, standing, lying down. Mix it up so that he gets used to hearing his name in a variety of situations. No matter the situation, you two will need this command obeyed. Before moving forward be certain your puppy knows and responds to his name being called.

~ Paws On – Paws Off ~

"Come", this command is important too

After your Poodle recognizes, and is responding to his name being called, then the "Come" command is the command that you want to teach next. Why? Because this one could save his life, save your sanity and save you running through the neighborhood in the middle of the night wearing little more than a robe.

Why, why do you do that? This is the best way to direct your dog into something else. If he is going for the trash, checking out the magic there, yell, "Come" and give him a reward when he does. Petting or play is a good reward for this one.

Here's what to do

- Once again, treat up. Find a quiet place so he can focus. Not the library, they are so picky about yelling in that place. Put a treat on the floor for your dog to eat and walk to the other side of the room. Next, hold out a hand with a new treat in it, say your dog's name to get his attention and give the command 'come'. Use a pleasant happy tone here. When he starts to come to you, praise him all the way to the treat. Do this about a dozen times and then take a break. You can also have help here, have a family member stand opposite you, and call your dog's name after you. Take turns calling your dog back and forth between you, doing this a dozen times.

- Next, start like before, treat on the ground, cross the room, call his name, and get his attention. This time, hold out an empty hand and give the command. Messing with him a little bit, but that is ok. As soon as he starts to come to you, praise him. When he gets to you, give him a treat from your pocket or pouch. Do this about a dozen times and then take a break.

- Keep practicing this with an empty hand, this is now a hand signal. You can take this another step by fading out the hand and just using the verbal cue.

Let's get complex

- Practice this exercise out of your dog's sight. Practice outside in increasingly more distracting situations. Start with the treat in hand, fade it to just the hand, then just to the words ... And then by email.

The Decoy Exercise, *Fetchus Interrupts* and Hide & Seek

- ***Decoy***; One person calls the dog; we will call him/her the handler. One person tries to distract the dog with food, and toys; we will call him/her the teaser. When the dog goes toward the teaser, they should turn away from the dog. When the dog goes toward the handler, he should be rewarded by both the handler and the teaser.

- ***Interrupting the Fetch***. Get a good-sized handful of his dry food. Now toss a ball or a piece of food. As your dog is chasing it, call him. If he comes AFTER he gets the ball/food, give him a little reward, one piece of food. If he comes BEFORE he gets the ball/food, give him a handful (7-10) of treats. After you've thrown the ball/food a few times, change it up, fake throwing something and call him, if he goes looking for the ball/food before he comes to you, small treat. If he comes immediately, give the huge treat. Try this with your teenage kids.

- ***Hide & Seek***. When you are outside and your dog is distracted and doesn't seem to know you exist, hide. When your dog comes looking for you, and finds you, reward him with lots of love and treats. Make it seem like an extremely big deal.

HELPFUL HINTS

- Never, call your dog for something he might find unpleasant. If you are leaving the park, call him, put on the leash and play a little more.

- Make sure coming to you is always the best thing ever. Always treat, praise and sometimes play with a ball or toy as an additional treat.

- You are calling, and your puppy is not responding, what now? Try this; run backwards away from him, crouch, and clap, show him a toy or food. When he comes, still reward him even though he stressed you out. In addition, run away from him, running towards him is a signal to play "catch me" and, unless you're an Olympic sprinter, you are not gonna win that one.

- Give him a treat when he checks in with you if he has been off the lead for a while.

- You should practice "Come" five to ten times a day, forever.

~ *Paws On – Paws Off* ~

"Drop it" – A must for all dog owners

Teaching your dog to drop it is very important. Why? Well, if you have young puppy you know that it is one giant mouth, everything goes into. Sometimes valuable and dangerous things go in it. Stephen Hawking actually got the idea of the black hole from his puppy's ever-consuming mouth. If you teach your dog right, when you give the command "drop it", he will open his mouth and drop whatever was in there, and importantly he will allow you to retrieve it. When teaching the drop it command you must make a good trade for what your dog has in his mouth. You need *to **out treat*** him, with a better treat. In addition, it is a good idea to stay calm and do not chase your puppy. Teach this command well, and your dog will be happy to hear the drop it commands. This command can also build trust. If you say drop it, retrieve and treat, your dog will know that you do not just steal things so he will *not guard* his favorite toys or food.

Teach "Drop It" Like This

- Gather good treats, the top-notch stuff, and a few items your dog might like to chew on; toys, rawhide, or socks. Treat in hand, encourage your dog to chew one of the items. When it is in his mouth, *put the treat close to his nose* and say, "Drop it". As soon as he opens his mouth, treat him as you pick up the item and then, return the item to him. Try this again. Now, your dog may not want to chew the item because there are treats in the area and he will want his mouth free for that. That is fine. Keep the treats handy, and throughout the day when you see him pick something up, practice the "Drop it" command. Do this at least ten times per day. Now, if he picks up a forbidden item, like Uncle Clumpy's wooden leg, you may not want to give it back to him. That is fine, just give him an extra tasty treat, take the leg away, and wipe the drool off before returning to Uncle Clumpy.

- Once you have done this treat to the nose 'drop it' command ten times, try it without the treat to the nose. Say the command and when he drops the item, give him a treat from your pocket or pouch. Make sure you give him extra treats the first time he drops it without the treat to his nose.

- Once you have done the above ten to twelve times, next move forward giving your dog something tasty, like a hard chew. Hold it in your hand and offer him the other side, do not let it go. For the love of all that's holy, do not let it go. Once he has it in his mouth, give the "Drop it" command. Give him extra treats the first time he drops it and offer the chew again. Repeat the exercise. Again, because better treats are possible, he may not take the chew back. That is OK go back to it later. Do these ten to a dozen times before you move to the next phase of 'Drop it'.

- Now repeat the exercise above, but this time do not hold onto the other side of the chew, let him have it. As soon as your dog has it in his mouth command "Drop it". When he drops it, give the treat AND give the chew back to him to keep. Oh, he will be thrilled. If he doesn't drop it, show the treat first (just a few times) and then work up to having him drop it before the treat appears.

- Once you have done this ten times successfully, try the command with things around the house he is not supposed to chew; toilet paper, chip bags, pens, gloves, and your shoes.

Then, try this outside where distractions are plenty. Gear up with the best treats when working outside and keep moving into further distracting situations. Your goal is to have the 'Drop it' command obeyed in any situation.

Know These Things

- If your dog already likes to grab things and have you chase him, start by teaching him you will not go chasing him. If he grabs and runs, ignore him. He will get bored and drop the item on his own. *Remember ignoring means sight, sound, and body language.*

- Try the command 'drop it' while playing fetch games.

~ Paws On – Paws Off ~

"Leave it", as opposed to "Drop it"

"Leave it" is a different command than 'drop it', you can tell by the spelling. The goal of the "Leave it" command is to get your Poodle's attention away from any object before it is in his mouth. This will keep him safe from dangerous objects like dropped medications, glass, wires or food of yours on the floor that is still within the three-second rule. Teach the "Leave it" command as soon as your dog recognizes his own name.

- Start with a treat in each fisted hand. Let him have a sniff at one of your fists. Give him the treat when he eventually looks away from the fist and has stopped trying to get the treat. When he does this, give him the treat from the OTHER hand. Keep doing this until he never tries to get the treat from your fist.

- Now, open your hand with the treat in it and show him, close it if he tries to get the treat. Do this until he simply ignores the treat in the open hand, the decoy hand. When he ignores it, give him the treat from the OTHER hand. Keep doing this until he ignores the treat in the open hand from the get go. When you have reached this point, add the command "Leave it". Open the decoy hand, say leave it, just once for each repetition, and then treat him from the other hand.

- Now put the treat on the floor and say, "Leave it". Cover it with your hand if he tries to get it. Treat him from the other hand when he looks away from the treat on the floor. Repeat this until he does not try to get the treat on the floor once you have given the command "Leave it". Repeat this.

- Now, try these steps; put the treat on the floor, say, "Leave it" and stand up. Treat if he obeys. Walk him by the treat on his leash, say, "Leave it". If he goes for it, keep him from getting it with his leash. Treat him when he ignores the treat. Increase the length of time between "Leave it" and the treat. Teaching him to 'leave it' with a treat first will allow you to build up to objects such as toys, animals, and people. You can build up to more and more difficult items with ease once he gets the idea in his head that "Leave it" means good things for him.

- After your dog is leaving the treat and other items, take training outside into the yard. Next, head to the dog park (where plenty of doodie lays that needs leaving) and other distracting places. Continue practicing daily until your dog has it down pat. This is another potential life saving command.

~ Paws On – Paws Off ~

Let's Sit

Teaching your dog to sit establishes human leadership, he knows who the boss is, and it is a perfect substitute for other problem behavior like jumping up on people. He will know what to do right away. Teaching him to sit is easy too.

- Find a quiet place and get your treats on. Wait until your dog sits down. As soon as his fuzzy rump hits the floor, give him a treat. Feed him while he is still sitting and then get him up again. Continue doing this until your dog is sitting right away after you reward treat him for sitting.

- Now, say, "sit" and just when he begins to sit and treat him. From here, only treat him when he sits after being told.

Try these variations for better sitting behavior.

- Practice five minutes a day in places with more and more distractions.

- Run around with your dog, play with a toy, and then ask him to sit. Reward him well when he does.

- Ask your dog to sit before you give him stuff he likes such as going outside, food, toys, and petting.

- Get him to sit in a variety of situations, such as, when strangers are around, when there is food on the table, outdoors, in the park, while you are speaking before a group of people.

~ Paws On – Paws Off ~

Handle Me Gently

Teaching your Poodle to be still, calm and patient while he is being handled is a very important step. It will make life easier for both of you at the groomer and the vet. It also helps with accidental bad touching and dealing with small children. This one will take patience and a few tricks to get it started. You can immediately begin to handle your new puppy to get him or her used to being handled.

Keep a few things in mind; Muzzles do not hurt dogs and they can be helpful and safe when he is learning to be handled. Easy cheese or peanut butter spread on the floor or the refrigerator door will keep him in place while he learns to be handled.

If he does not like to be handled, he can learn to accept it. You must practice this with your dog one to three minutes a day so that he becomes comfortable. This is a life-long process.

With all of the following exercises, follow these steps:

- Begin with short, non-intrusive good touching. If he is calm and he is not trying to wiggle away, treat him up.

- If he wiggles, keep touching him but do not fight his movements, keep your hands on him lightly and move with him. When he settles, treat him and release him.

- Do not go on to another step until he ENJOYS the current one.

- Don't work these exercises more than a few minutes at a time. He could become stressed out.

Handling Different Areas of the Dog's Body

The Collar

Find a quiet place to practice, get treats.

- Touch his collar under his chin and release him right away while you treat him. Do this ten times or until your dog is happy with it.

- Hold the collar under his chin for 2 seconds, treat, and repeat. Increase the amount of time until you hit ten seconds. Treat after each elapsed amount of time.

- Hold the collar under his chin and give it a little tug. If he accepts this, does not resist, treat, and repeat. If he wiggles, keep a gentle hold on the collar until he calms down, and then treat and release him. Repeat this step until he is happy with it. Now, switch to the top of the collar and repeat the whole progression. Remember to increase the time held and the intensity of the tug very slowly. Pull/tug but do not jerk your dog's neck and head.

Paws in the clause

It is a fact that most dogs do not like to have their paws touched. Go slow with this one so your dog enjoys it and keep touching his paws the rest of his days. In the following exercises, if he does not wiggle and try to get away, treat him up. If he does wiggle, stay with him gently keeping contact, and treat and release when he calms down. Each one of these steps will take a few days to complete and will require a dozen repetitions. Make sure you complete each step and your dog is happy before you go on to the next one. *Do each step with all four paws, and pause between paws.*

- Pick up his paw and immediately give him a treat. Repeat this five times and then progress adding one second each time.

- Hold the paw for ten-seconds.

- Hold the paw and move it around.

- Massage the paw.

- Pretend to trim the nails.

Side Note: Do not trim your dog's nails unless you absolutely know what you are doing. It is not easy and it can cause extreme pain to your dog if you screw it up.

Do you ear what I ear? (Good luck getting through Christmas now)

- Reach around the side of your dog's head and touch his ear. Treat and repeat ten times.

- Once, he is good with this, practice holding the ear for one-second. If he is calm, treat. If he wiggles, stay with him until he is calm, then treat and release. Do this until you can reach ten seconds with no wiggling.

- Manipulate his ear. Pretend to clean the ear. Go slow so that your dog enjoys it. It will take a few days so practice until your dog is calm for the ear cleaning part. If your dog is already sensitive about his ears being touched, it will take longer. Go Slowly.

From the mouth of dog's

- Gently touch your dog's mouth, treat, and repeat ten times.

- Touch the side of his mouth and lift a lip to expose a tooth. Treat and release only when he is not resisting.

- Go slowly now with these. Lift the lip to expose more and more teeth on both sides of the mouth, and then open the mouth. Treat and release when he does not resist.

- Touch a tooth with a toothbrush then work up to brushing his teeth for one to ten-seconds.

A tell of the tail

Many dogs and servers are sensitive about having their tails handled, and rightly so.

- Start by briefly touching his tail. Repeat this ten times with treats until he is good with it.

- Increase the time you hold his tail until he is good with ten-seconds.

- Go slowly through these steps; pull the tail up, brushing the tail, giving the tail a gentle tug.

Children, nuff said

You must prepare your poor dog to deal with the strange, unwelcome touching that is often inflicted on them by children. Alternatively, you could put a sign around his neck that says; "You must be at least 18 to touch this dog". However, it is very likely that you will encounter children that are touchy, grabby, pokey children.

- Prepare your dog for the strange touches children may perpetrate. Prepare him by practicing and treating him for accepting these odd bits of contact like ear tugs, tail tugs, a little harder than normal head pats, kisses, and hugs. Keep in mind, as we said before, dogs and kids are not a natural pairing. Even a dog that is "good with kids" can be pushed to a breaking point and then things can get ugly.

Always supervise children around your dog. ALWAYS!

Can you give me a lift?

An emergency may arise that requires you to lift your dog. Practice this slowly. First, put your arms around him briefly. Give him a treat if he stays still. Increase the time. Next, slowly proceed to lifting off the ground and back down, treats when he does not wriggle. Increase the time and the distance you lift him. Prepare him for the groomer or the vet by lifting him up and placing him on a table.

The brush off

- Get your dogs brush and lightly touch him with it all over his body. If he remains unmoving, treat and repeat. Repeat this until you can brush his whole body and he does not move. You can get your dog comfortable with all varieties of touching and handling if you work slowly, patiently and with good treats. It is a very important step in his socialization to get him comfortable with being handled.

~ *Paws   On   –   Paws   Off* ~

Going Out On a 'Leash' Here

Training your Poodle to the leash is probably one of the hardest things you will do. However, in the end, it is very rewarding and can strengthen trust and the bond between you and your dog. There is a variety of collars to choose from, do some research, and figure out which one is best for your dog. Head collars and front attachment harnesses are a couple of choices. Make sure it fits right, the leash is not too long, he is comfortable in it, and other dogs are not mocking him. The main goal here is to get your dog to walk beside you without pulling against the leash. An easy way to prevent that is to stop moving forward when he pulls and to reward him with treats when he walks beside you. The following steps will you train your dog to have excellent leash manners. Loose leash walking is the goal.

Walking With You Is A Treat (Step the first)

Put a non-retractable leash on your dog, ten to 20 feet long. Load up with the top notch treats, meat or cheese and head out to the back yard or familiar, quiet outdoor spot. Decide whether you want your dog to walk on the left or the ride side of you and you will always give him his treat at the thigh of that side you chose. Soon he will be coming right to that side because it is Treatsville.

Start walking randomly around the yard. When your dog decides to walk with you, give him a treat at the thigh of your chosen side. If he continues to walk with you on the correct side, give him a treat with every step the two of you take together. Keep practicing this until your dog is staying by your side more often than not. Do not worry about the treats; you will eventually phase them out when he learns this behavior.

Eyes on the THIGHS (Step the second)

Start walking around the yard again and wait for your dog to lag behind or get distracted by something else. Say, "Let's go" to him, clap or slap your thigh to get his attention. Make sure you use a cheerful, welcoming tone. When he pays attention to you, walk away.

- If he catches up with you before the leash gets tight, treat him from your thigh on the chosen side. Treat him again after he takes a couple of steps with you.

- If he catches up after the leash gets tight do not treat him, say "Let's go" again then treat him after he takes a couple of steps with you.

- If he does not come when you say, "Let's go" and the leash is tight, stop walking and give some gentle pressure to the leash. When he begins to come toward you praise him. When he gets to you, do not treat him, rather say, "Let's go" again. Treat him if he stays with you and keep treating him for every step he stays with you.

- Keep practicing this step until he is staying at your aide while you walk around the yard. If he moves away from you say, "Let's go" to recall him, and then treat him.

Oh the things to smell and pee on (Step the Third)

Just like you, your dog is going to want to sniff things and go potty. I hope that you do not do this in your neighbor's yard. When he is on the leash, every five minutes or so, when you would normally treat him, instead say "go sniff", "go play", "carouse", something, and let him have some free time on the leash. Keep in mind this is a form of reward so if he pulls on the leash during this time say, "Let's go" and walk the opposite direction, ending free time quickly and cleanly.

Where's the BOSS? (Step the Fourth)

Continue practicing leash walking in the yard same as steps one through three. Gradually, shorten the leash until you have only a 6-footer going. Change direction, change speed, and treat him every time he is able to stay with during the changes. Now when he is used to walking by your side you can start phasing out the treats. Do treat him when he does something difficult like keeping up with the changes.

Michael McDonald time (Taking it to the streets)

Now take your dog out of the back yard and onto the sidewalk for his daily walk. You will apply the same techniques as you did in your back yard, only now you have to deal with more distractions. Now, you will be dealing with other dogs, friendly strangers, squirrels, traffic, who knows what else. Arm yourself with the special treats, be patient, and go slow. Use the "Let's go" command when he pulls his leash or forgets that you exist. Give him treats when he walks beside you. Moreover, do not forget *sniff breaks*, those are rewards too.

Stop and Go exercise

Have a 6-foot leash attached to the collar. Hold the leash and toss a treat or a toy about twenty feet ahead and start walking toward it. If he pulls the leash and tries to get the treat, use the "Let's go" command and walk the opposite direction of the treat. If he stays beside you while you walk toward the treat let him have it as his reward. Practice this several times until he no longer pulls toward the treat but stays at your side. Remember you should control sniffing and potty stops.

TROUBLE SHOOTING

- If your dog is crossing in front of you make your presence known to him. He may be distracted.

- If he is lagging behind you, he might be frightened or not feeling well. Give him a lot of encouragement instead of pulling him along. If the lagging is due to sniffing or potty, keep walking. In this case, apply only gentle pressure to the leash.

- Remember, lots and lots of rewards when he walks beside you.

Heel

This is a good command to teach your dog when you walk him by distractions, other dogs, traffic, noise, etc. You want to keep your dog close to you so he doesn't get into trouble.

- Start by putting a treat in your fist on the chosen side of your body. Let him sniff the fist and say "heel". Take a few steps leading him along with the treat in your fist at your thigh. Treat him when he is following your fist with his nose.

- Next, have him follow at your side with an empty fist. Treat him when he follows your fist for a couple of steps.

- Continue to practice heel and up the ante, the length of time before you treat him, moving around, changing direction and the like.

- Now, try this outside and more distracting situations.

~ Paws On – Paws Off ~

Supine Time (Lie Down)

Teaching your dog to lie down helps to keep him in one place, calms him down, and it is useful to replace barking.

Basics – "Down"

- Get in that quiet place with lots of treats. Wait for your dog to lie down of his own will and then give him a treats while he is lying down. Toss a treat to get him up again. Keep doing this until he lies down directly after he gets the second treat.

- Now, as soon as he starts to lie down say "Down", and treat him. From here on, only treat him when lies down on your command.

- Next, practice this in other places, different distracting areas, around strangers, wearing a hat (you or the dog). Be patient in the more distracting locations.

PROBLEMS SOLVED

- If he will not lie down, try teaching him, no joke, in the bathroom. Unless your dog likes decorative bath soaps, and he may, there is not much to distract him in the bathroom.

- If he does lie down but pops right back up, give him his treat in the lying down position as often as possible.

~ Paws On – Paws Off ~

"Stay" (Just a Little Bit Longer)

Self-control and practical uses such as keeping him from bolting out the door, waiting for you, and jumping on people. 'Stay' is a great command to teach your dog. This is an easy command to teach after you have taught him "Sit" and "Down".

- Get to a quiet place with treats. Give the "Sit" command, but wait two-seconds before you treat him. Continue this until he will sit for ten seconds before a treat comes to him. **Begin to use the phrase "Sit- Stay"** when you treat him. When you switch to "Stay", add a hand signal. This should be your flat hand about a foot or so from his little face.

- If he gets up, it means you are moving too quickly. Say to yourself "my bad" and try again with a shorter stay time goal. Build it up slowly, like courage before confessing about that tattoo.

- Take one healed step away from your dog and treat him for staying. Keep going until you can take two steps in any direction. Make sure you go back to him to treat him. *Do not* let him come to you for a treat.

- Keep doing this until you can take several steps and be out of sight. Work until you can get him to stay for a two full minutes while you are in his sight. When you have this down, combine the two.

- Now, try all this starting with the "Down" command.

HELPFUL HINTS

- Vary the difficulty; your dog might not decide to play if it keeps getting harder and harder all the time.

- Always, reward him where he stayed. Do not release him with a "come" command and then treat him. Mixed signals, no one likes those.

Practice "Stay" regularly before you give him his food bowl, before he meets a new person, before he goes out the door or he goes to the prom on that big night out.

~ Paws On – Paws Off ~

Go West Young Dog, or, Wherever Else I Point You

"Go" is a great cue to get your dog into his crate, the car, off the couch. This is a very handy command to send your dog to a spot.

- Find a quiet place, treats, and your dog. Place a towel on the floor. Put a treat in your hand and use it to lure your dog to the towel while saying, "GO". When all four paws are on the towel, treat him up. Do this about ten times.

- Start the same way as above but this time, empty handed. When all four paws are on the towel ten times, treat him while on the towel.

- Keep practicing with the empty hand and eventually turn it into a pointed index finger. Also, repeat ten times.

- Now, cue with "Go" while pointing to the towel but do not walk to the towel with him.

- Now, try this on different surfaces and other places, off the couch, in and out of his bed, etc. Practice this in more and more distracting situations.

One Step Beyond – Settle

This is teaching your dog to go to a mat and lie on it until she is released. This is for when you need your dog out of your hair for extended periods.

- Put a mat on the floor. An actual mat, not your neighbor named Matt. Although – tempting.

- Give the "Go" command and treat her when she has all four paws on the mat. While she is on the mat, issue the command "Down - Stay". *Go to* her and treat her on the mat.

- Now, give the "Settle" cue and repeat the above exercise.

- Give the "Settle" cue and wait for her to go to the mat and lie down before you treat her. Do not use any other cues.

- Make it more difficult; vary distance, distractions, and time in settle mode.

~ *Paws On – Paws Off* ~

Nipping, Yep, the Ole Nipperdoggie

Friendly puppies nip for a few reasons; they are teething, playing or they want to get your attention. My Uncle Dexter nips from a bottle, but that is a completely different thing. Not to worry, most puppies will grow out of this behavior naturally. Other herding dogs nip as a herding instinct to round up their animal charges or family members.

While he is working through the nipping stage, you want to avoid punishing or correcting your dog, this could strain your relationship down the line. You also want to teach your puppy how delicate human skin is. Let him test it out and give him feedback. Say 'yipe', 'youch', or 'bowie' and pull your hand back when he bites too hard. If you act more and more sensitive to the nips, he will get the fact that humans are VERY sensitive and respond accordingly with his teeth.

This is a very easy behavior to modify because we know the motivation behind it. The puppy wants to play and chew and who doesn't? Give him a lot of chew toys and when he nips, walk away, and ignore him. If he follows you and nips at your heels, its tie up, time out time. Then, when he is gentle, stay and play with him. Use patience my friend, patience, this will pass in time.

Preventing the Nippage

- Have a chew toy in your hand when you are playing with your puppy. This way he learns the right thing to bite and chew.

- Get rid of your puppy's excess energy by exercising him *at least* an hour a day. He will have no energy to nip.

- Make sure he is getting enough rest and he is not cranky. 12 hours a day is good.

- Have lots of interesting chew toys around to help your puppy through the teething process.

- Do not leave kids and dogs unattended. I have said this before and it should be repeated. Also, teach your kids not to run away screaming from nipping puppies. They should walk away quietly and stop moving.

Instructing Around the Nippage

- Tie your puppy back or put him in a room with a gate that you can get over quickly.

- Play with him and praise him for being gentle. When he nips say, "*yipe*" like a puppy would and quickly walk away.

- Wait one minute and return to give him another chance. Practice this for two or three minutes and give everyone who will have daily contact with the puppy, family, roommates, a chance to play and train as well.

- This method also works well for other attention getting behavior like jumping, barking, and the dreaded leg humping.

~ Paws On – Paws Off ~

Jumping Jeepers

Your dog loves you and wants as much attention from you as possible. The reality is that you are his world. If he is sitting quietly, he is easily forgotten. When he is walking beside you, you are probably thinking about other things, work, the car, anything but the loyal companion beside you. He gets your full attention only when he jumps up on you. Then you look at him, shout at him, and push him down until he is down on the floor. Then, you ignore him again. What do you expect? He wants your attention. Teaching your dog not to jump is essentially teaching him that attention will come only if he has all fours on the floor.

Now, it is important as you teach your Poodle not to jump, that you do not punish him. Don't shout "No" or "Bad". Do not knee him or push him. The best way to handle the jumping is to turn your back and ignore him. Remember, since he loves you very much your dog or puppy may take any contact from you as a positive sign. You do not want to send mixed signals.

For the jumping practice, it would be great if you could gather at least ten people. You want to train your dog to understand that he will only get attention if he is on the ground. If you cannot acquire ten people, do not take it personally, remember what mom said, if these ten people don't like you, you'd find ten others that do. If ten people are not available, then teach him to remain grounded using his family. When he encounters other people, use a strong "Sit - Stay" command to keep all four paws planted firmly.

No Jumping On the Family

This is the easiest part because the family and frequent visitors have more chances to help him learn. When you come in from outside and your dog starts jumping, say, "oops" and immediately leave through the same door. Repeat this after a few seconds. When he finally stops jumping when you enter, give him a lot of attention. Ask the rest of the family to follow the same protocol when they come into the house. If you find that he is jumping at other times besides when you enter, like when you sing karaoke, just ignore him by turning your back and put energy into giving him attention when he is sitting.

No Jumping on Others

Prevention is the key to this exercise, especially with larger dogs. You can prevent him from jumping by using a leash, a tieback, crate, and gate, or if you are up for the challenge, use the force, Luke. Until you have had enough practice and your dog knows what you want him to do, you really should use one of these methods to prevent him from hurting someone or getting an inadvertent, petting reward for jumping. To train, you will need some dog training volunteers and infrequent visitors to help.

Guests Who Wants to Help Train Your Dog (Thank you in advance)

- At home, the guest comes in the door, the dog jumps, they say "oops" and leave immediately, just like you did with your family. Practice this with at least five different visitors, each making multiple entrances in the same visit. Completely ignore your dog.

- On the streets: Have your dog on a leash. The guest will approach your dog. If he strains against the leash or jumps, the guest turns their back and walks away. When your dog calms himself and sits, the guest approaches again. Repeat this until the guest can approach, pet and give attention to your dog without your dog jumping. Have the volunteer repeat this at least five times.

- Make a tieback, attach an extra leash to something sturdy, within site of the doorway but not blocking the entrance. Keep this there for a few months. When the guest arrives, hook your dog to the secure leash and then, let the guest in.

- Once your dog is calm, the visitor can greet him if they wish. If the guest does not wish to greet your dog, give him a treat to calm his behavior. If he barks, send him to his crate or the gated time out area. The goal is that you, *not your dog*, always greet guests first.

- If he is able to greet guests calmly while tied back, then he may be released. Hold the leash the first few times just to be sure.

A Caveat to These Two Methods

1) Teach your dog that crossed arms means the same as the command sit. By combining the word "Sit" with a crossed arm gesture, he will learn this. Ask your guests, the ones who want to help train him, to simply cross their arms, and wait until your dog sits before they pet him. This will help you with people who unintentionally do things to get your dog so excited, such as wave their arms, jump up and down or sing, "I'm so excited".

2) For those who do not want to help teach your dog when someone enters the house, treats are tossed six to ten feet away from that person. Keep treats by the door and toss them when the person comes in. He will eventually anticipate this and stay away and off the person. When he has calmed down a bit, ask him to sit and then, give him some good attention.

~ Paws On – Paws Off ~

House Training

Fact is, dogs are a bit particular about where they "potty" and will build a very strong habit. When house-training your Poodle it is important to prevent accidents because whenever she goes 'potty' in the house, she is building a strong preference to that particular area. When your dog does relieve herself in the house, *blame yourself*. Until your Poodle has learned where she is supposed to do her business, you should keep a constant, watchful eye on her whether she is in her crate or on a mat.

- If she is having accidents in the crate, it may be too big. The crate should be big enough to stand up, turn around, and lay down in.

- When she is inside, out of the crate, watch for sniffing or circling, as soon as you see this behavior, take her out right away. Do not wait.

- Set a timer to go off every hour so that you remember to take her out before nature calls. With progress, you can increase the time.

- If she does not do her 'duty' when you take her out, bring her back in, keep a close eye on her, and try again in 15-minutes. Could be that she got shy. We have all been there!

Schedule This

You should take your puppy out many times during the day, most importantly after eating, playing, or sleeping. Feed her two or three times per day and leave the food down for around 15-minutes at a time. Your younger dogs, (also known as puppies) can generally hold for a good 1-hour stretch. For adult dogs, do not go longer than 8 hours. In the beginning, bring your puppy outside often. This avoids accidents in the house and gives her more chances to receive rewards from you for doing what you want her to. You can keep water down until about eight at night then remove from your puppies reach.

Consistency Is the Mother of Prevention

Until your dog is reliably house-trained, bring her to the same spot each time and leave a little bit of her waste there. This will be the potty spot. Hang a sign if you'd care too, something tasteful that you get made at a renaissance fair. Use this spot for pottying only, not play. Bring your puppy to her spot and say something like "Hurry Up" when you see her getting ready to go. As she is going, say nothing, this distracts her, but when she finishes, praise her, pet her and give a top-notch treat. Spend about five minutes or so playing with her too, not at the potty spot. If he does not go, take her inside, keep an eye on her, and try again in 15 minutes.

If she goes in the house, remember, that is *your fault*. Maybe you went too quickly with the training or were not clear enough about the potty spot. If you see her relieving herself in the wrong spot, bring her quickly outside to the potty spot, when she is done, praise her for finishing there. If you find a mess, clean it really well without your puppy watching you do it. Use a cleaner specifically for pet stains so there is no smell or evidence that you failed her – (again kidding- *but you knew that*)– so that way, it will not become a regular spot for her, or a new regular chore that you need to clean up.

This Question Rings a Bell: Can I Teach Him To Tell Me When He Needs To Go Out?

Yes, you can. Hang a bell, at his level, by the door you use to take your dog outdoors. Put some peanut butter on the bell. When he touches it and rings it, open the door immediately. Repeat this every time you take him to the potty spot. Eventually, he will ring the bell without the peanut butter. Now he will tell you when he needs to go outside. Be careful here, he may start to ring the bell when he WANTS to go outside to play or explore, or just, go outside and not have to potty. To avoid this, each time he rings the bell, take him out to the potty spot ONLY. If he starts to play, take him in immediately.

Small Dogs often take long to potty train. I really do not know why, they just do. One way to help is to take them out more often than you would a larger dog. The longest I would go without taking a small dog to the potty spot is about 4 hours. In addition, many small dogs do well with a litter box. This way, they can go whenever nature calls and whatever the situation, such as when there is a blizzard outside and they refuse to get their tiny paws cold. Remember now, do not call him a "Cat", he will not feel respected.

~ Paws On – Paws Off ~

Care and Goals, Being a Good Human to Your Dog

Chow Time

- Low Quality Foods: Stay away from corn, wheat, by products, artificial preservatives, and artificial colors. (Also, anything in the 'eetos' food group, Cheetos, Doritos, burritos, and mosquitoes)

- Avoid junk food. It helps if you do not teach the Poodle how to dial the phone and order a pizza. Consult your veterinarian if you need specific diet guidance for your dog.

Go to: Dog Nutrition

Handling

- Your Dog is comfortable being touched on paws, ears, tail, mouth, entire body, and this is practiced daily.

Go to: Handle Me Gently

Basic Care

Oral maintenance, clipping, and other grooming will depend upon you and your dog's activities. We all know our dogs love to roll and run through all sorts of possible ugly messes, and put obscene things into their mouths, then afterward run up to lick us. Below is a list of the basic grooming care your dog requires. Pick up a grooming book on your specific breed so that you know what and how often your dog needs particular services, extra care areas, and what you may need to have done by professionals.

Most basic care can easily be done at home by you, but if you are unsure or uncomfortable about something, get some tutelage and in no time you will be clipping, trimming, and brushing like a professional.

Coat Brushing - Daily brushing of your dogs coat can be done, or a minimum of 4-5 times a week depending upon your breed's coat. Some breeds blow their coat once or twice a year and daily brushing is recommended during this period. Many breeds do not require daily brushing but it is still healthy for the coat and skin.

Some Equipment: Longhaired dogs need pin brushes, short, medium, and some longhaired dogs need bristle brushes. Slicker brushes remove mats and dead hair, rubber curry combs polish smooth coats, clippers, stripping knives, rakes, and more or less depending upon your dog's coat.

Bathing - Regular but not frequent bathing is necessary. Much depends upon your breed's coat. Natural coat oils are needed to keep your dogs coat and skin moisturized. Never bathe your dog too frequently. Depending upon what your dog has been into, once month is adequate. Bathing should be done at least once per month, with warm water and a gentle shampoo or soap made for dogs.

Nail trimming - For feet health, your dog's nails should be kept short. Special clippers are needed for nail trimming. Start when your dog is a puppy and most likely, you will have no issues, but if your dog still runs for the hills or squirms like an eel, then your local groomer or veterinarian can do this procedure.

Ear cleaning - Clean your dog's ears at least once a month depending upon your breed but inspect them every few days for bugs such as mites, and any odd discharge. Clean the outer ear only. Use a damp cloth or cotton swab doused with mineral oil.

Eye cleaning - Use a moist cotton ball to clean discharges, and avoid putting anything irritating into your dog's eyes.

Brushing teeth - Pick up specially designed canine tooth brushes and paste. Clean your dog's teeth as frequently as daily. Try to brush your dog's teeth a few times a week at minimum. If your dog wants no part of having his or her teeth brushed, try rubbing his teeth and gums with your finger. Next, put some paste on your finger, let him or her smell/lick it, and repeat rubbing the teeth and gums with your finger. Then repeat with the brush. Keep plenty of chews around that promote healthy teeth. When your dog is 2-3 years old, he or she may need their first cleaning.

Anal sacs - These sacs or located on each side of a dog's anus. If you notice your dog scooting his rear, licking, or scratching his anus, the anal sacs may be impacted. You can ask your veterinarian how to diagnose and treat this issue.

Doing Things: Fun and Educational

- To avoid doggy boredom, make sure you have many toys for your dog to choose from the toy bin. This could include a Nylabone™, and or a Kong™ dog chews, ropes, balls, and tugs. Your more advanced breeds might enjoy mahjong, air hockey, or play station.

Be sure your Dog is:

- Comfortable with human male and female adults.

- Comfortable with human male and female children.

- Comfortable with special circumstance people, for example, those in wheel chairs, with crutches, braces, or even strange "Uncle Larry".

To assure that your Poodle *isn't* selfish, make sure that he or she is:

- Comfortable with his food bowl, toys or bed being touched by you or others.

- Comfortable sharing immediate space with strangers, especially children. This is necessary to socialize so that he doesn't get paranoid or freak out in small places, for example, elevators in Hollywood filled with celebrities and their handbags, or at the next door neighbors house.

- Comfortable sharing his best friend, YOU, and all family members and friends.

For road trippn' with your Poodle, make sure he or she is:

- Comfortable in a car, truck, minivan, or in a form of public transportation.

- Always properly restrained.

- "Knows how to operate a stick shift as well as an automatic."

In general, a happy Poodle should have the following:

- It is suggested to provide at least 10 hours of sleep per night in an adult's bedroom, but not in your bed, in your dogs own bed or mat.

- Regular health checks at the vet, and all of his vaccinations, including rabies and distemper. Read up before agreeing on extra vaccinations. Avoid unnecessary vaccinations or parasite treatments.

- Be neutered or spayed.

- Proper weight of your dog is that you should be able to feel his ribs but they do not stick out.

- Plenty of playtime outside and with proper supervision.

~ *Paws On – Paws Off* ~

Barking Madness

Dogs bark for many reasons, most commonly, for attention. Your dog may bark because he wants to play or get up or he wants you to feed him. Whatever the case, DON'T DO IT, do not give your dog attention for barking. Say, "Leave it" and ignore him. YOU do not want him to learn that barking works, that if he barks, he gets you moving. Ignore him, do not look at him, and go to the other side of the room. Make it clear to your dog that barking does not work. In the end, make sure you are initiating activities he likes and make them happen on YOUR schedule. Show your pup who is in charge as often as possible. Also, make sure that he earns what he gets. Have your pup sit before he gets the reward of going outside to play, getting his leash put on, his bowl of food, or for that matter Red Sox tickets or *Le Miserable* (should THAT apply more aptly) .

He may bark when he hears or sees something interesting. Here are some ways to deal with that.

When You Are Home

- Prevent it. Block the source of sound or sight. Use a fan or blinds or simply put him in a different area of the house.

- Teach him "Quiet". When your dog barks, wave a piece of food in front of his nose. When he stops barking to sniff, treat him right away. After doing this about three times, the next time he barks, pretend you have a piece of food and say "Quiet". Treat him as soon as he stops barking. Treat him again every few seconds he remains quiet after hearing the cue. Eventually, you can increase the time lapse between cues and treats.

- Reward him for being quiet on his own when he hears or sees something that would usually make him bark.

The Time Out

You can use a "Time Out" but do not use it too often. When you give your dog a T/O, you are taking him out of his social circle and giving him what is known as a negative punishment. This kind of punishment can have side effects that we do not want to teach him. Side effects like him learning that you walking towards him are a bad thing. The T/O should be used very sparingly and to emphasize teaching your dog the behavior that you prefer and preventing bad behavior.

- Decide where you want the time out spot to be, a place that is not the same as the potty spot or the dancing spot. It should be somewhere that is not scary, not wonderful, but it is safe, maybe a gated pantry, or the bathroom. If your dog or puppy does not mind his crate, you can use that. Have your dog wear a 2-foot piece of rope. When your pup barks, using a calm voice command "Time Out", take the rope, and walk him firmly but gently to the T/O spot. Leave him there for about 5 minutes. When he is calm and not barking you can release him. You may need to do this few times before he understands which behavior has gotten him the time out.

When You Are Not at Home

- Again, prevent barking by blocking the sounds or sights that cause it. Use the fan, blinds or keep him in another part of the house.

- Use a Citronella Spray Collar. Only use this for when you cannot take the barking anymore. Do not use this when the barking is associated with fear or aggression. You will want to use this a few times when you are home with him first so he understands how it works.

On A Walk

When you are walking your dog, he may bark at other dogs, people, cars, critters, out of excitement.

Here are some helpful tools to defuse that behavior.

- Teach him "Watch me". Start in the house with fewer distractions. Say your dog's name and "Watch me" while you hold a treat to your nose. Treat him when he looks at the treat for once second.

- Practice this ten times and then practice while pretending to have a treat, you will make this a hand signal.

- Build the length of time he can continue to watch you.

- Now practice "Watch me" while you are walking around inside. Then practice outside. Practice it outside near something he finds interesting. Practice in a situation he would normally bark. Perhaps at the studio when composing his next hit.

Other Solutions

The "Quiet" command is for when he begins to bark or you notice something that would make him bark. Command "Quiet", and give him a treat. Treat him every few seconds that he remains quiet. Teach him that his barking triggers mean "Quiet". For example, if he barks at cars. When a car goes by, put a treat by his nose, and then bring it to your nose. When he looks at you, treat him. Repeat this until he voluntarily looks at you when a car goes by and does bark, and then treat him.

- You can also treat him for calm behavior. When you see something or encounter something that he would normally bark at and he does not, treat him.

- Flee! If he has not yet learned the quiet cue while you are out walking or he just doesn't respond to it, simply turn around, and walk away from the thing that is making him so excited. Treat him when he calms down.

- Use the citronella spray collar if you cannot take the barking anymore but only when the barking is NOT associated with fear or aggression.

He is Afraid, Aggressive, Lonely, Territorial, or Hung-over

He may have outbursts when he feels any of these things. You should first try to prevent outbursts by crating, gating, blocking windows, using fans to hide sounds and avoid taking him places that cause these outbursts, the park, the sidewalk by a busy street. This is not a permanent solution; it is simply helpful when you are teaching him he does not have to be afraid. Do this for about 7 days before starting training to allow his body and mind a chance to be calm.

SOME TIPS

- Remain calm.

- If it is too much, you may want to hire a professional positive trainer for private sessions. When doing so, tell her / him to first read my eBook, and then follow it verbatim :)

Get your dog to change his mind about what he is upset. Teach him that, what he was upset about before now predicts his favorite things. Here is how.

- When the trigger appears in the distance, treat him. Keep treating him as you get him closer to the trigger. If he is territorially aggressive, teach him the doorbell or knock means he gets in his crate and waits for treats. You can do this by ringing the doorbell and luring him to his crate and giving him treats.

- You can also lure him through his fears. If you are walking and you encounter one of his triggers, put a treat to his nose and lead him out and away from the trigger zone. On the other hand, if you are Kenny Loggins ... Take him right out of the danger zone.

- Use the "Watch me" command when you see him getting nervous or afraid. Treat him frequently for watching you.

- Reward Calm behavior.

He Is Bored and Frustrated

He may get bored or frustrated because he can sense he is not making you happy. At these times, he may lose focus, not pay attention to you, and spend time writing bad poetry in his journal. Here are a few things that can *help prevent this.*

- Keep him busy and tire him out with chew toys, exercise, and training.

- He should have at least 30 minutes of aerobic exercise per day, maybe a private step class. In addition to the aerobic exercise, he should have 1 hour of chewing and about 15 minutes of training. Keep nice varieties coming. It is, after all, the spice of life.

He Is Excited to Play

Like an actor in the wings, your puppy will get excited about play. Teach him that when he starts to bark, the play stops. Put a short leash on him and use it to lead him out of play sessions if he barks. Put him in a "time out" or just stop playing with him. Reward him with more play when he calms down.

~ *Paws On – Paws Off* ~

Body Language and Vocals

Training your dog seems like a daunting task, but it is a unique and rewarding experience. It is the foundation of a healthy and long relationship with your new dog or puppy. You must be the one in charge of the relationship and lead with the pack leader mentality, all the while showing patience and love. Whether you choose to enroll your dog in an obedience school such as the Sirius reward training system or go it alone at home, you will need assistance via books, videos, and articles to help guide you through the process and find solutions to obstacles along the way.

Without a doubt, it is nice to have an obedient friend by your side through good times and bad. Owning a dog is a relationship that needs tending throughout the years. Once you begin training, it will continue throughout the life of your dog and friend. An obedient dog is easier to care for and causes less household problems and expense. You know what needs to be done, but what about your dog. How do you read his messages in regards to what you are attempting to accomplish? I am going to cover dog's body language and verbal language to provide insight into what it is your dog is trying to tell you. This should prove to be an asset while training your dog.

Body Language:

What is body language? Body language is all of the non-verbal communication we make when engaged into an exchange with another entity. Say what? All of the little tics, spasms, and movements we act out comprise non-verbal body language, and studies state that over 50% of how people judge us consists of our body language.

Meaning the visual interpretation of our message is equal to our verbal message. This is interesting; when the body language disagrees with the verbal, some studies have stated that as little as 7-10% of our verbal message accounts for how the others judge us. With that kind of statistic, I would say that body language is extremely important.

Similar to humans, dogs use their bodies to communicate. Their hearing and seeing senses are especially acute. Observe how your dog tilts his head, moves his legs, and what his tail is doing. Is the tail up, down, or wagging? These body movements are all part of the message your dog is trying to convey. With this knowledge, I think it is safe to say that we should learn a little about human and dog body language. In this article, I will stick to a dog's body language and leave the human investigation up to you. What do you think my posture is right now?

The Tail:

The tail is a wagging and this means the dog is friendly, or maybe not. With most dogs that have tails it can convey many messages, some nice, some nasty. Specialists say a dogs wagging tail can mean the dog is scared, confused, preparing to fight, or be confident, concentrating, interested, or happy.

How do you tell the difference? Look at the speed and range of motion in the tail. The wide-fast tail wag is usually the message of "Hey, I am so happy to see you!" wag. The tail that is not tight but sticking straight back, or close too, means the dog is curious but unsure, and probably not going to bite but remain in a place of neutral affection, (Verdict is not in). This dog will probably not be confrontational.

The slow tail wag means the same; the dog is gauging the friendly meter as to friend or foe. The held high and stiff, or bristling (hair raised) tail is the **WATCH OUT!** *'Red Flag'* for humans to be cautious. This dog may not only be aggressive but dangerous and ready to rumble. If you come across this dog, it is time to calculate your retreat and escape plan.

Not only the speed and range of the wag should be recognized while reading the doggie body language. One must also take note of the tail position. A dog that is carrying its tail erect is a self-assured dog in control of itself. On the flip side of that, is the dog with their tail between their legs, tucked in tight. The tucked tail is the "I surrender man, I surrender, please don't hurt me" posture. This applies to humans and its fellow K-9's. The chill dog, a la Reggae special, is the dog that has her tail lowered but not tucked in-between her legs. The tail is just down and relaxed stating the dog is the same.

While training your dog or simply playing, it is a good idea to take note of what his or her tail is doing and determine if your dog's tail posture is matching his moods. Your understanding of your dog's tail movements and posture will be of great assistance throughout his lifetime.

Up Front:

In the front end of the dog lie the head and ears with their special motions. A dog that cocks her head or twitches her ears is giving the signal of interest and awareness, but sometimes it could be fear. The forward or up ear movement dictates the dogs awareness of seeing or hearing something new. Due to the canines sense of hearing being amazingly acute this can occur long before we are aware. These senses are two of the assets that make dogs so special as well as fantastic watch guards.

"I give in, and will take my punishment" is conveyed with the head down and ears back. Take note of this submissive posture, observe the neck, and back fur for bristling. Sometimes this accompanies this posture. Even though a dog is giving off this submissive stance, it should be approached with caution because it may feel threatened and launch an offensive attack thinking he needs to defend his self.

"Smile, you are on camera." Yep, you got it, dogs smile too. It is usually a subtle corner pull back to show the teeth. Do not confuse this with the obvious snarl that entails a raised upper lip and bared teeth, sometimes accompanied by a deep growling sound. The snarl is something to take stock of and be extremely cautious. A snarling dog is not joking around the snarl is serious. This dog is ready to 'throw down'.

The Whole Kit and Caboodle:

All in message delivery, using the entire body, a dog that rolls over onto her back and exposes her belly, neck, and genitals is conveying the message that you are in charge. A dog that is overly submissive will sometimes urinate a small amount to express her obedience towards a human or another dog.

Front paws down, rear end up, tail is a waggin, "Hut, hut, hut, C'mon Sparky hike the ball", this posture is the ole K-9 position of choice for "Hey, it is playtime, and I am ready to go". This posture is sometimes accompanied with a playful bark and or pawing of the ground in an attempt to draw you into her playful state. I love it when a dog is in this mood, albeit they can be aloof to commands.

Whines, Growls, Howls, Barks and Yelps. Sounds Dog's Make and We Hear

We just had a look at silent communication in body language, now I will look into the doggie noises we cherish, but sometimes find annoying. Just what is our dog trying to tell us? Our K-9 friends often use verbal expression. Whines and growls mean what they say so when training your dog listen carefully. As you become accustomed to the dogs verbal communication and are able to begin understanding them, the happier you will both become. Some dog noises may be simply annoying and keep or wake you up, these may need to be trained as inappropriate to make your dog stop.

Barking:

What does a dog bark say and why bark at all? Dogs bark to say "Hey, what's up dude" or "Look at me", warn of trouble, and to convey that they are bored or lonely. I think we all know that stimulated and excited dogs also bark. It is up to us to survey the surroundings and make a decision of the reason. We need to educate ourselves about our dog's barks so we can act appropriately.

Whining and Whimpering:

Almost from the time they are freshly made and feeding upon their mother's milk our little puppies begin to make their first little fur-ball noises. Whimpering or whining to get their mothers attention for feeding time or comfort, they know mom will come to them. They also use these two W's on us to gain our attention. Other reasons for whimpering or whining are from fear produced from hearing loud noises such as thunderstorms and fireworks. I think most of us have experienced the 4th of July phenomenon of the entire dog population going at it until the wee hours of the morning when the last firework is ignited, and the final "BOOM!" dies off.

Growl:

Growling means, you better watch out, and are acutely aware of what the dog is doing, and might do. Usually a dog that is growling is seriously irritated and preparing to be aggressive.

Howl (And Not the Poem):

Picture the dark silhouette of a howling dog with the full moon backdrop. A dog's howl is a distinct sound that many K-9 make and all wolves make. Howling can mean loneliness, desire, warning, or excitement. A lonely howl is a dog looking for a response. "Is anyone out there" – Pink Floyd. Dogs also howl after a long hunt when they have tracked and cornered their prey.

A Couple of Things Regarding Training Your Dog:

Knowing what you want to train your dog to do is as important as training your dog. A puppy is a blank slate and knows no rules, so it is a good idea to make a list and have an understanding of what you would like your puppy to do. As he grows, the same principle applies and you may adjust training from the basics to further topics like making a good travel, hiking, or hunting dog and companion. What conditions you plan to expose your dog or puppy to outside of the household may require different training tactics as well as exposure to circumstances that will allow him to be ready for those encounters.

~ Paws On – Paws Off ~

Dog Treating

Treats, treats, TREATS! Come and get em'. How many times have you heard a friend or family member tell you about some crazy food that their dog loves? Dogs do love a massive variety of foods; unfortunately, not all of the foods that they think they want to eat are good or great for them. Dog treating is not rocket science but does take a little research, common sense, and paying attention to how your dog reacts after wolfing down a treat.

I am going to throw out some treats for training as well as some regular ole "Good Dog" treats for your sidekick and friend in mischief. I will touch on the proper time to treat, giving the treat, types, and bribery vs. reward.

Types of Treats

Love and attention is considered a reward, treat as positive reinforcement, and can be just as effective as an edible treat. Dog treating is compromised of edibles, praise, love and attention, as well as play or allowing some quality time with their favorite piece of rawhide. At times, these treats are crucial to dog training.

Human foods safe for dogs such as fruit and veggies, cut up meats that are raw or cooked, yogurt, peanut butter, kibble, and anything you come up with that your pup loves, but is good for him and his digestive system are all great for dog treating. Not all human foods are great for dog treating though, please read up regarding human foods that are safe for dogs.

Giving the Treat

Try to avoid treating your dog when he is over stimulated and running amuck and in an unfocused state of mind. This can be a counterproductive treating as it may reinforce a negative behavior or you may be unable to get your dogs attention.

When giving the treat allow your dog to get a big ole doggie whiff of that tasty food treat, but keep it up and away from a quick snatch and grab. Due to their keen sense of smell, they will know long before you figure it out that there is a tasty snack nearby. Issue your command and wait for him to obey before issuing the doggie reward. Remember when dog treating to be patient and loving, but do not give the treat until he obeys. Try to use the treating to reward the *kickback* mellow dog not the out of control or over-excited dog.

Some dogs have a natural gentleness to them and always take from your hand gently, other dogs need some guidance regarding taking the treat from your hand in a manner that is gentle. If your dog is a bit rough on the ole treat grabbing hand, go ahead and train the command "Gentle" when giving treats. Be firm that from this point forth no treats will be given unless taken gently. Being steadfast with this decision will work well and soon your pup or dog will comply if he wants his tasty treat.

Time to Treat

The best time to be issuing dog treats is in between his or her meals. If training always keep the tastiest treat in reserve in case you need to reel your dog's attention back to the training session. Too close to meal times all treats are less effective so keep that in mind when planning you training sessions. Obviously if your dog is full from mealtime he will be less likely to want a treat reward than if he is a bit hungry, therefore your training session is apt to be more difficult and far less effective.

What's In the Treats?

Take a gander at the treat ingredients and makes sure there are no chemicals, fillers, additives, colors and things that just seem unhealthy. Certain human foods that are tasty to us do not go down the doggie palette too well so take note. Almost all dogs love some type of raw meat and or slightly cooked meats. In tiny nibble sizes, they work great to get their attention where you want it focused.

Many people like to make homemade treats and that is fine, just keep to the rules we just mentioned and watch and read what you are adding while you are having fun in the kitchen. Remember to read the list of vegetables dogs can and cannot eat, and note that pits and seeds cause dog's issues such as choking and intestinal issues such as gas. Remove the seeds and pits, and clean all fruits and veggies before slicing into doggie size treats.

Bribery vs. Reward Dog Treating

The other day a friend of mine mentioned bribery for action when he wanted his dog to shake his hand. I thought about it later and thought I would clarify. **Bribery** is offering the food in advance to get the dog to act out the command or behavior. **Reward** is giving your dog his favorite toy, food, love, affection after he has performed the behavior.

Example of bribery - you want your dog to come and you hold out in front of you a huge mound of steak in your hand before calling him. Reward would be giving your dog

the steak after he obeyed the "Come" commar
to you.

Bribed dogs learn to comply with your wishes only when they see food, the rewarded dog realizes that he only gets his reward after performing the desired action. This is also good as other non-food items can more easily be introduced as rewards when dog treating.

~ Paws On – Paws Off ~

Dog Nutrition

Nutrition, humans study it, practice it, complain about it, but usually give into the science of it. The same as humans, dogs have their own nutrition charts to follow, different theories, scientific studies and so forth.

Together, let's look at history, common sense, raw foods, nutrient lists, and what your dog might have to bark about regarding what he is ingesting and thinks he can and cannot eat.

In the beginning there were wild packs of dogs everywhere, and what did they eat anything that they could? Similar to humans survival; dogs depended upon meat from kills, grasses, berries, and other edibles that nature provides. Guess what the great news is? Many millennia later nature is still providing all that we need.

Some History

In Roman history, the Romans wrote about feeding their dogs barley bread soaked in milk along with bones of dead sheep. The wealthy Europeans of the 1800's would feed their dogs better food than most humans had to eat. Dead horsemeat was oft rounded up from the streets to recycle as dog food to the rich estates on the outskirts of the city. Royalty is legendary for pampering their dogs with all sorts of delicacies from around their countries and elsewhere. Meanwhile, the poor's dogs had to fend for themselves or starve. Being fed table scraps from a pauper's diet was not sufficient to keep a dog healthy, and the humans themselves often had their own nutrition problems. Dogs would hunt rats, rabbits, mice, and any other rodent type creature they could sink their teeth.

Other references from the 18th century tell of how in France the French would mix bread crumbs with tiny piece of meat, or mix the liver, heart, blood, or all, with milk or cheese along with bread for feeding dogs. In England, they would also offer meat flavored soups to their canines to add to their dog's nutrition.

In the mid to late 1800's a middle class blossomed out of the industrial revolution. They started taking on dogs as house pets and created the enterprise of feeding the household pets that were suddenly in abundance. This new class with its burgeoning wealth had extra money to spend. Noting that the sailor's biscuits kept well for long periods James Spratt began selling his own recipe of hard biscuit for dogs in London, and soon after took his fare to New York City. It is believed that he started the American dog food business. This places the dog food and kibble industry at only a bit over a 150 years old, and now is a multi-billion dollar business

All the while we know that any farm dog, or for that matter, any dog that can kill something and eat it will do just that. Nothing has changed throughout the centuries. Raw meat does not kill dogs, so it is safe to say with some common sense and diligence a raw foods diet will not either.

Raw Food Stuff

Let us take a look-see at the raw food diet for canines. First remember our dogs, pals, best friend, comedy actors, were meant to eat real foods such as meats, either cooked or uncooked. Their DNA is not formed only to eat dry cereals concocted by men in white lab coats. These cereal and canned foods may have been keeping our pets alive, but possibly not thriving at optimum levels.

There are many arguments for the benefits of real and raw foods. Sure it is more work, but isn't their health worth it? It is normal, not abnormal to be feeding your dog, a living food diet; it is thought that it will really boost their immune system and over-all health. *All foods* contain a risk, dry, wet, or raw they can all contain contaminants or parasites.

There are different types of raw food diets. There are raw meats that you can prepare at home, freeze-dried, and frozen that you can easily thaw and feed your dog.

Raw food diets are foods that are not cooked or sent through a processing plant. Only you can decide what you think is the type of diet for your dog, but it is worth the research effort to read up on a raw foods diet or mix of kibble and raw foods.

Rules of thumb to follow for a raw food diet

1. Before switching make sure your dog has a healthy GI track.

2. Be smart and do not leave meat un-refrigerated for lengthy periods.

3. To be safe simply follow human protocol for food safety. Toss the smelly, or does not seem right meats and foods.

4. Keep it balanced. Correct amount of vitamins and minerals, fiber, antioxidants, and fatty acids. Note medical issues and correlation.

5. Gradual switch over is often recommended to let their GI track adjust. Use new foods as a treat then watch stools to see how the dog is adjusting.

6. Take note of the size and type of bones thrown to your dog. Not all dogs do well with real raw bones.

7. Freezing meats for three days, similar to sushi, can help kill unwanted pathogens.

8. Take notes about what is working and not working with your dogs systems. Remember to be diligent in observation and note taking to track new diet.

9. Like us humans, most dogs do well with different foods. There is no one size fits all diet.

10. Please read up on raw foods before switching over, and follow veterinary guidelines.

~ Paws On – Paws Off ~

Human Foods for Dogs

There are many human foods safe for dogs. In reality, human and dog foods were the same for most of our existence. Well, maybe we wouldn't eat some of the bugs, and vermin they eat, but if we were hungry enough we could. Whether you have your dog on a raw food diet, partial raw food diet, or dog foods, you can still treat with some human foods. Even a top quality dog food may be lacking in some nutrients your dog needs, also a tasty safe human food such as an apple can be used as a treat in training. Below is a short list of some safe human foods to feed your dog. As usual, proceed in moderation to see how your dog's digestive system reacts and adjusts to each different food. Always keep plenty of clean fresh drinking water available for your dog.

Short List of SAFE Human Foods for Dogs

Oatmeal

Oatmeal is a fantastic alternative human food source for grain for dogs that allergic to wheat. Oatmeal's fiber can also be beneficial to more mature dogs. A general set of rules can be followed when feeding your dog oatmeal. Limit the serving sizes, and amount of serving times per week, be sure to serve the oatmeal fully cooked, and finally never add any sugar or additional flavoring.

Apples

REMOVE the seeds. There's not much better in human foods safe for dogs to crunch on than apples. My dog loves to crunch on apples. Apples offer both vitamin C and Vitamin A for your dog. They are a good source of fiber for a dog of any age. Caution, do not let your dog eat the seeds of the apple OR the core as they are known to contain cyanide. A few will not be detrimental, so do not freak out if it happens. Just be cautious and avoid the core and seeds.

Brewers Yeast

After alcohol is made, what is left over is 'Brewers Yeast'. It has a tangy taste that dogs will clamber over. B vitamins can be found in the yeast, which is great for the dog's skin, nails, ears, and coat. Do not use 'baking yeast' as it is altogether different than 'Brewers Yeast' and can make your dog become ill if eaten. All you need to do is add a couple of sprinkles on your dog's food to spice it up. Experiment a few times to test your dogs taste for spice.

Eggs

Does your dog need a protein boost? Eggs can help because they contain protein, selenium, and riboflavin in them that is easily digested. Cook your egg(s) before serving your best buddy, because he or she will actually get more of the proteins needed. Eggs are good for energy and strength and great for training as well.

Green Beans

A Lean dog is a happier, more energetic dog. Feeding your dog green beans is a good source of manganese, and vitamins C and K, and is considered a good source of fiber. If you have a lazier dog living 'A Dog's Life' then it is good to be proactive with your dog's weight. Add a steady stream of fresh green beans in your dog's diet for all the right reasons. Avoid salt.

Sweet Potatoes

Vitamin C, B-6, manganese, beta-carotene, and fiber can be found in sweet potatoes. Slice them up and dehydrate and you have just found a great new healthy source for treating your dog. Next time you are out shopping for potatoes, pick up sweet potatoes, and see if your best little buddy takes to them. My bet is that your dog will love them.

Pumpkins

A pumpkin is a fantastic source of vitamin A, fiber, and beta-carotene. Trend towards a healthy diet with plenty of fiber and all the essential vitamins and proteins your dog needs. Pumpkin is one way to help you mix it up a bit. Feed it dried or moist, separate as a treat, or with his favorite bowl. Pumpkins can be a fantastic fun alternative natural food for dogs.

Salmon

A great source of omega 3 fatty acids, salmon is a fish that helps your dog's immune system, its skin, coat, and overall health. Some dog owners notice an increases resistance to allergies. Be sure to cook the salmon before serving it. You can use salmon oil too. For treats, added flavoring, a whole meal, or added flavoring, salmon is a fantastic source of human foods safe for dogs.

Flax Seed

Grounded or in oil form, flax seed is a nourishing source of omega 3 fatty acids. Omega 3 fatty acids are essential in helping your dog maintain good skin and a shiny healthy coat. Note; you will want to serve the flax seed directly after grounding because this type of fatty acid can go turn sour soon after you do. Flax seed is also a wonderful source of fiber your dog or puppy needs.

Yogurt

Always a great source for your dog's calcium and protein, yogurt is another one of our top ten human foods safe for dogs. Pick a fat free yogurt with no added sweeteners, or artificial sugar, color or flavoring.

Melons

Great for your dog, are watermelons, cantaloupes, honeydews, but check regarding other exotic melons.

Peanut butter

Yep, a big spoon full and it will also keep him occupied for a while.

Berries (fresh & frozen)

Blueberries, blackberries, strawberries, huckleberries or raspberries provide a tasty snack.

Cooked chicken

Chicken sliced up and yummy for your K9 to enjoy in addition, or in place of his regular meal.

Cheese

Sliced cubed pieces are great for training or in place of food, or a tablespoon of cottage cheese on top of your dog's food.

Bananas

All fruits have phytonutrients, and required nutrients that are beneficial to your canine.

Carrots

Crunchy veggies are good for the teeth

UNSAFE Human Foods

Below is a list of harmful foods for dogs. This is not a complete list, but a common list of foods known to be harmful to our k9 friends. If you are unsure of a food that you wish to add to your dog's diet, please consult a veterinarian or expert on dog nutrition.

Onions: Both onions and garlic contain the toxic ingredient thiosulphate. However, onions are more dangerous. Many dog biscuits contain *small* amounts of garlic, which contains less of this toxin so large amounts would need to be consumed to be toxic. This poison can be toxic in one large dose, or with repeated consumption that builds to the toxic level.

Chocolate: Contains theobromine, a compound that is a cardiac stimulant and a diuretic. This can be fatal to dogs.

Grapes: Contains an unknown toxin that can affect kidneys.

Raisins: (Same as above)

Most Fruit Pits and Seeds: Contains cyanogenic glycosides resulting in cyanide poisoning. The fruits by themselves are OK

Macadamia Nuts: Contains an unknown toxin.

Most Bones: Should not be given (especially chicken bones) because they can splinter and cause a laceration of the digestive system and/or become lodged in your pet's throat. They also pose a choking hazard.

Potato Peelings and Green Potatoes: Contains oxalates, which can affect the digestive, nervous, and urinary systems.

Rhubarb leaves: (same as above)

Broccoli: (*only toxic in large quantities*)

Green parts of tomatoes: Contains oxalates, which can affect the digestive, nervous, and urinary systems.

Yeast dough: Can produce gas and swell in your pet's stomach, leading to a rupture of the digestive system.

Coffee and tea: (due to the caffeine)

Alcoholic Beverages: Could lead to coma or even death.

Human Vitamins: Especially vitamins containing *iron*, which can cause damage to the lining of the digestive system, kidney, and liver damage.

Moldy or spoiled foods: There are many possible harmful outcomes from spoiled foods.

Persimmons: These can cause intestinal blockage.

Raw Eggs: Salmonella.

Salt: In large doses can cause an electrolyte imbalance.

Mushrooms: Can cause liver and kidney damage.

Avocados:

Xylitol: This artificial sweetener is not healthy for dogs.

~ Paws On – Paws Off ~

According to nutritional scientists and veterinarian health professionals, your dog needs twenty Amino Acids, yet ten of which are essential. At least thirty-six nutrients and a couple of extra may be needed to combat certain afflictions. Your dog's health depends upon the intake of the following nutrients.

36 Nutrients for dogs:

1. 10 essential Amino Acids – Arginine, Histidine, Isoleucine, Leucine, Lysine, Methionine. Along with Phenylalanine, Threonine, Tryptophan, and Valine.

2. 11 vitamins – A, D, E, B1, B3, B5, B6, B12, Folic Acid, and Choline.

3. 12 minerals – Calcium, Phosphorus, Potassium, Sodium, Chloride, Magnesium, Copper, Manganese, Zinc, Iodine, and Selenium

4. Fat – Linoleic Acid

5. Omega 6 Fatty Acid

6. Protein

Suggested Daily Quantities of Recommended Nutrients		
Nutrient	Puppies	Adult Dogs
Protein (%)	22.0	18.0
Arginine (%)	0.62	0.51
Histidine (%)	0.22	0.18
Isoleucine (%)	0.45	0.37
Leucine (%)	0.72	0.59
Lysine (%)	0.77	0.63
Methionine + cystine (%)	0.53	0.43
Phenylalanine + tyrosine (%)	0.89	0.73
Threonine (%)	0.58	0.48
Tryptophan (%)	0.20	0.16
Valine (%)	0.48	0.39
Fat (%)	8.0	5.0
Calcium (%)	1.0	0.6
Phosphorus (%)	0.8	0.5
Sodium (%)	0.3	0.06
Chloride (%)	0.45	0.06

We realize it may take time to understand what will make your dog thrive as far as diet is concerned. When daily feeding your dog, do your best to include all thirty-six nutrients mentioned here. All of which can come from fruits, veggies, kibble, raw foods, and yes, even good table scraps. You will soon discover what your dogs preferred foods are. For your dog to maintain optimum health he needs a daily basis of a healthy GI track, well rounded diet, a good balance of exercise, rest, socializing, care, and love.

~ Paws On – Paws Off ~

That's All Folks

Well, that is about all I have in writing for you today. Believe me, it is not everything. Training your Poodle is a lifelong endeavor. There are other methods, tricks, tools, and things to teach him and learn with him. You are never done, but it is half of the fun of having a dog.

Remember, to think like your dog and to always be patient with your dog and with yourself. If you do this right, you have a relationship and a bond that will last a lifetime. You will have joy and friendship like none other. If you do this wrong, you will have misery and ulcers. *Not really* but, it is better to do it right. Keep this book handy and reference it often. In addition, look for other books including mine, ask friends what they have experienced, and keep broadening your training skills. This will serve to keep you and your Poodle happy and healthy for a long, long time.

Thanks for reading. I hope you enjoyed this as much as I have enjoyed writing it and training my dog!

~ Paws On – Paws Off ~

DON'T THiNK – BE, ALPHA DOG

I wrote this book to inform and instruct dog owners of the fundamentals for establishing and maintaining the *alpha* position within the household hierarchy. Inside the book you will learn how to live, lead, train, and love your dog in a **non-physical 'alpha dog' way**. Leading from the *alpha* position makes everything dog related *easier*. All dogs need to know where they are positioned within the family (pack), understand, and trust that their *alpha* will provide food, shelter, guidance, and affection towards them. Then life becomes *easier* for you and your dog.

Whether you are reading this before, after, or during reading one of my "Think Like a dog..." breed specific training books, I know this will assist and guide you while training and owning your dog companion, *because* with these 'alpha' fundamentals your dog will obey your commands in critical situations, and follow your lead into a safer and happier life. Having an obedient dog keeps other animals and humans safe.

A dog that respects his 'alpha' leader is easier to control, teach, and trust. He is more likely to obey your commands and respect your rules. Be the 'alpha' now.

~ Paps

"**Alpha Dog Secrets**" by Paul Allen Pearce

LEARN MORE:

http://www.amazon.com/dp/B00ICGQO40

Hey...Did I miss something?

STUMPED?

Got a Question about Your Poodle?
Ask an Expert Now!

Facebook ~
https://www.facebook.com/newdogtimes

NewDogTimes ~
http://newdogtimes.com/

It's where the **Poodle Secrets** have been hidden -since their Ancestral Wolf Packs were forced to collide with Man...

Wait Until You Learn This!

About the Author

Paul Allen Pearce is the author of many breed specific "Think Like a Dog" & "Think Like Me" dog-training books, "Alpha Dog Secrets Revealed", and others. When his family duties allow, he spends his spare time outdoors with his two dogs Buck and Samson. He lives in the South Eastern part of the United States.

Think Like a Dog - But Don't Eat Your Poop!

Visit us today!

Share Our Links – Like us, Pin us, Feed it, Tweet it and Twerk it – We Need Help Too!

Facebook ~

https://www.facebook.com/newdogtimes

NewDogTimes ~

http://newdogtimes.com

"Thanks for reading. I hope you enjoyed this as much as I have enjoyed writing it and training my dog!"

"Keep on training and loving your Now Zen Like 'Kung-Fu' dog. Please be patient, loving, and have fun while training your dog."

~ Paul Allen Pearce
~ Paws On – Paws Off ~

LEARN MORE:

http://www.amazon.com/dp/B00ICGQO40

Poodle Facts

Country of Origin: Germany, standardized in France.

Other Names: Caniche, Barbone, Chien Canne, French Poodle, Pudle.

Nicknames: N/A

Group: Non-Sporting, Toy.

Purpose: Water retriever.

Size: Large and small.

Height: Standard - over 15in (38cm) Miniature - over 10 but under 15 inches (28-38cm) Toy - 10 inches (28cm) or under.

Weight: Standard - 40 to 55 pounds Miniature - 12 to 15 pounds Toy - 5 to 10 pounds.

Lifespan: 14 to 18 years.

Colors: Blues, greys, silvers, browns, cafe, apricots, creams, and parti colored with patches over white, and phantom, which is the same coloring as the Doberman Pinscher.

Coat: Single layer of dense, curly fur, ranging from coarse, woolly to soft, and wavy. Their hair can be corded similar to human dreadlocks, but most people brush and clip Poodle coats and there are many designs. Coat clipping every 6-8 weeks. Inspect ears regularly. Clipping required due to shedding hair remaining trapped inside the coat.

Shedding: Little that leaves the dogs body

Odor: Minimal

Apartment: Yes, relatively inactive indoors. All three versions need proper exercise, and the Standard and Miniature do best with at least a small yard.

Temperament: Active, highly intelligent, elegant, good-natured.

Exercise: Long daily walks at a minimum, add play, and running. The Standard and Miniature love water and enjoy a good swim. For optimal mental and physical health, they need their daily exercise.

Training: Highly trainable, enjoy learning and performing, ranked #2 in Stanley Coren's "The Intelligence of Dogs meaning that in most cases this breed learns and retains in less repetitions than almost all other breeds. Lead from the alpha position with a firm, confident, and calm manner. Poodles are sensitive to vocal tones so take note to keep an even tone and temper. Once you have earned their respect as the leader they will comply efficiently.

AKC Quick Facts

- The denominations Standard, Miniature, and Toy are used to describe size only. All the Poodles are one breed, governed by the same standard.

- The Toy Poodle is known for superior intelligence and exceptional learning ability.

- The Poodle clip is not merely decorative (though it may seem that way now); it is in fact a necessary clip meant to protect the joints and vital organs in cold water.

- The Toy Poodle achieved great popularity in France and was known worldwide as a "trick dog." They were court favorites during the reign of Louis XVI and Queen Anne.

- The Toy Poodle, like all Poodles, possesses wonderful swimming ability; the coat is adapted to water, and will cord if left to grow naturally.

- Grover Cleveland owned a Poodle (although some reports say it was a Pekingese)

Other Books

"Don't Think BE Alpha Dog Secrets Revealed"

"Think Like a Dog...but don't eat your poop!"
(Breed specific dog training series)

"Think Like Me...but don't eat your poop!
(Breed specific dog training series)

Legal Disclaimer:

The author of **"Think Like a Dog…but don't eat your poop!, Paws On ~ Paws Off books** Paul Allen Pearce is in no way responsible at any time for the behavior of your pet, not now or in the future. Animals, without warning, may cause injury to humans and/or other animals. Paul Allen Pearce is not responsible for attacks, bites, mauling', nor any other viciousness or any and all other damages. We strongly recommend that you exercise caution for the safety of self, the animal, and all around the animals while working with your dog. We are not liable for any animal or human medical conditions or results obtained from training. While all attempts have been made to verify information provided in this publication, neither the author nor the publisher assume any responsibility for errors, omissions or contrary interpretation of the subject matter contained herein. The publisher and author assume no responsibility or liability whatsoever on the behalf of any purchaser or reader of the material provided.

CPSIA information can be obtained
at www.ICGtesting.com
Printed in the USA
BVOW06s1151030817
491050BV00010B/46/P